# PART OF THE SCENERY

## Also by Mary Wesley

### NOVELS

Jumping the Queue

The Camomile Lawn

Harnessing Peacocks

The Vacillations
of Poppy Carew

Not That Sort of Girl

Second Fiddle

A Sensible Life

A Dubious Legacy

An Imaginative Experience

Part of the Furniture

### CHILDREN'S BOOKS

Speaking Terms

The Sixth Seal

Haphazard House

# PART OF THE SCENERY

## *A Celebration of Life in the West Country*

Mary Wesley

Photographs by Kim Sayer

BANTAM PRESS

LONDON · NEW YORK · TORONTO · SYDNEY · AUCKLAND

TRANSWORLD PUBLISHERS
61–63 Uxbridge Road, London W5 5SA
a division of The Random House Group Ltd

RANDOM HOUSE AUSTRALIA (PTY) LTD
20 Alfred Street, Milsons Point, Sydney,
New South Wales 2061, Australia

RANDOM HOUSE NEW ZEALAND LTD
18 Poland Road, Glenfield, Auckland 10, New Zealand

RANDOM HOUSE SOUTH AFRICA (PTY) LTD
Endulini, 5a Jubilee Road, Parktown 2193, South Africa

Published 2001 by Bantam Press
a division of Transworld Publishers

A catalogue record for this book is available
from the British Library.
ISBN 0593 047176

Printed in Great Britain by
Butler & Tanner Ltd, Frome

1 3 5 7 9 10 8 6 4 2

# CONTENTS

# A WRITER
## *and Her Sources*

As I was chatting one day with two friends, one a writer, the other a photographer, we discovered that we had all three, though none of us native to the West Country, decided for similar reasons to settle in it with our families and to take root. This part of the world is a very good place to work in, especially for freelances such as ourselves. London, with its publishers, libraries and galleries, is within reach though not distractingly near. The countryside is beautiful, its inhabitants friendly, the climate damp but liveable.

Was our work influenced by our environment, the writer, James Long, asked us, and if so, how much? His, it seemed, was not affected at all but mine, he suggested, was hugely influenced and he cited *The Camomile Lawn*, *Harnessing Peacocks* and *Part of the Furniture* for starters. 'And you,' he said to the photographer, 'are never without your camera.' Kim Sayer readily agreed. I told them that my love of the West Country, and Devon and Cornwall in particular, had started when I was a small child living near Salcombe, in a cottage at South Sands, a cove close to the mouth of the Kingsbridge estuary. Kim said he knew the area well for he had spent all his holidays there and that was why, when he and his wife decided to leave London, they had moved to where they live now – in a house looking down onto the Dart estuary and across country to the long line of

ABOVE
Sennen Cove, a tremendous stretch of pale sand. When my children were very small they had the beach to themselves as it was wartime.

LEFT
On the beach at South Sands.

Dartmoor in the distance and the high hump of Haytor. James then suggested that we should visit South Sands to see how much it had changed since I lived there in 1918, before he and Kim were born. We had lunch there and for me the visit brought back a flood of memories of a childhood I would presently write about here. Kim started taking photographs of the coast – not much changed – and his interest grew so that he asked about the other places where I have lived in Devon and Cornwall. Then we began to make expeditions together.

While he took photographs, I tried to locate the settings which have been reworked in my books to create a pastiche of this lovely country I have lived in for the best part of fifty years. Some of the places have been built up and developed but the beaches and coves, the cliffs and Dartmoor in particular are as lovely, wild and unspoilt as they were when as a small child I began to explore them.

This book is a reminder of people and events both real and imaginary, happy and sad, which have been part of my life and little pieces of which have got themselves woven into my work.

# On Writing

When I was a child I told myself stories, as children do. I can remember my elder sister asking, 'Where are you now?' by which she meant what reign, what period, what century had captured my imagination. Was I living in the era of the French Revolution, a companion to Sir Percy Blakeney? With the children of the New Forest? With David Balfour and Alan Breck Stewart in *Kidnapped* perhaps? Never with Sir Walter Scott's lot, he was too long-winded, and never rubbish like *The Swiss Family Robinson*. Nor did Pierre Loti appeal or Charlotte M. Yonge get a look in. My sister soon took to painting; I went on dreaming, did not lose the habit and from time to time, as I grew into adolescence, I wrote, and when I was about sixteen I secretly decided to be a writer. What I wrote I have long forgotten. Whatever it was, it was written to please myself, then consigned to the wastepaper basket.

Once I unwisely told a boyfriend that I still invented long sagas. I was grown up, already married, and we were driving back to London from a wedding in the country. 'Huh!' he said. 'You should have grown out of that by now!' Not long ago – we are both in our late eighties – I reminded him of this put-down.

Early in the Second World War I wrote a short novel making fun of the people who were streaming nervously out of London to avoid air raids which had not yet begun. I lost the manuscript. Soon afterwards I myself, pregnant and not allowed

Myself at twenty-five.

The lane down to Cullaford Cottage.

to stay in London, went with the baby I already had to live in Cornwall with a friend who was also pregnant, for the rest of the war. I took to writing in bed. The house we lived in was draughty and extremely cold. I went early to bed where I spent the long anxious nights listening to music on my radio – ironically the German stations were wonderful – and reading and writing.

I was reading Synge, Rainer Maria Rilke, C. S. Lewis and, best of all, T. S. Eliot. I suspect that the poems I wrote were, at their best, parodies of Eliot. I threw them away but Eric Siepmann, whom I later married, must have seen one or two, for when in 1944 he went to Paris and met Louis Aragon he sent me 'Les Yeux d'Elsa' and asked me to translate it. Tucked up in a four-poster bed with a pile of books, my radio, a wind-up gramophone and a dog at my feet, I wrote short stories, poems and a diary which I now rather wish I had not consigned to the hot-water boiler, and of course letters.

On the beach at Shaldon in Devon.

From my bed I could hear the wind whoosh and roar through the belt of Mediterranean pine which protected the house and the sea thump its great waves against the rocks half a mile away and planes, German and British, drone overhead. This atmosphere of war I used when writing *The Camomile Lawn* and *Part of the Furniture*, though in neither book were the houses I wrote about anything other than figments of my imagination, real only to me.

The war over, I lived with and then married Eric Siepmann. Now I was given every encouragement to write, for Eric was a journalist and a writer himself and he understood the urge. But bringing up children, looking after a husband, keeping house, coping with animals, cooking and cleaning filled my days and

Cliffs at Land's End.

*'Come, Ducks, run.' Sophy raced up the hill with the delighted dog, arriving abruptly on the camomile lawn. She ran round it, brushing the turf with her feet. It was the wrong time of year and the scent was faint. She stopped running and looked at the sea, rough and grey, sea horses turning into rollers to crash against the cliffs. She looked along the path, blocked by barbed wire, to the coastguard station once so bravely white, now camouflaged dirty green and brown. 'It's all gone,' she cried miserably to the dog, who whimpered, feeling the wind sharp and cruel on his thin coat.*

The Camomile Lawn

there would be times when, unable to find either the necessary hours or the privacy, I would despair. I can remember taking to my bed, pretending to be ill – 'Don't come near me, I'm infectious' – and writing, just to get it out of my system for a while, to give myself pleasure, to find release.

It was my husband who eventually put an end to my reclusiveness, made me find an agent, stopped me throwing away, urged me to get published. He had, until then, been the only

person allowed to see anything I wrote. He was immensely encouraging, hugely generous.

When my children's book *Speaking Terms* was accepted by Faber & Faber he wept with joy, and again when Macdonald published a strange sort of science fiction book, *The Sixth Seal*. I had set it on Dartmoor, thinking of Thornworthy, and used the moor and the river Dart and invented a town, a cross between Dartmouth and Fowey.

The snow-covered moor above Fernworthy Forest.

## Growing Up in the Country

Throughout my writing life I have drawn upon my memories of the countryside I knew as a child. Farmers were very kind to children when I was young. In those days farms were safe places. Not so now with all the machinery, immense black plastic bags full of hay which have been known to roll and kill a child, and drums containing chemicals for the sprays used six to eight times on crops before they are harvested (and digested by us). I was born when a haycart was not much different from Constable's haywain, when horse power worked the land and

A thorn tree twisted by the gales.

every farm gave employment to a number of men. Nowadays farming is a solitary job, where finances oblige most people to work alone and employ a series of contractors.

Right up to the 1950s, shire horses pulled the plough. The same horses were harnessed to the haycarts and brought in the corn. Horse power was plodding and slow, but it got the jobs done and was lovely to watch. I know one farmer on the Land's End peninsula in Cornwall who still runs his farm with horses and he does very well. Long may he last.

As a small child I haunted the farms. I scattered corn for the chickens and geese and I fed the ducks. I was allowed to fetch the cows in from the fields for milking with the farm dogs. I learned to milk (until after the Second World War practically all milking was done by hand). A farmer's wife taught me to make butter in a churn when I was seven. I made friends with the pigs. Farmers were very relaxed, very kind. There was no danger that I was aware of. They laughed when I rode on a cow. (It was very uncomfortable.) They sat me high up on the carthorses. They let me drive the carts. (The horses knew the way anyway.) I leaped and bounced with other children on the hay and watched the making and thatching of haystacks. I even tried to ride the pigs, and this, if you can stay on, is an art in itself as a pig does not like to have a child on its back.

We were country children in spirit, I suppose, although we lived for long spells in the city. Even in London, until well into the 1920s there were horse-drawn carts and shops such as Harrods, Selfridges and United Dairies had very snappy delivery vans. Scott's the hatter, I remember, ran a particularly smart outfit.

Myself aged five.

I discovered when I learned to ride, aged about seven, that the best view you can get is from a horse's or pony's back. Many of the lovely photographs of the moors in this book are views I have seen from on top of a horse.

Riding on moorland has a particular charm and a unique sound which, with the subtle creak of leather and the horse's breathing, is of your horse's feet brushing through the heather. On horseback you are not a threat to wildlife. You can get quite close to otherwise timid birds; once I was lucky enough to watch the lovemaking of weasels. And there is the added bonus of the smell of horse, which I happen to love.

I was taught to ride by an Exmoor pony. My mother put me on her. 'You hold the reins like *this*,' she said. 'You keep your heels down, your hands down and sit up straight' – and that was about all I got from my mother. She had taught my brother and sister to ride, could not be bothered a third time, and was candid enough to say so.

My brother had but to sit on a horse for it to rush backwards, and he took to fishing and shooting instead. My sister became a formidable and fearless rider who hunted and went in for eventing. My riding has always been of a gentle, ambulatory nature that enables me to look at the view.

My teacher, Jenny the Exmoor pony, was kind. When I fell off – which was often – she would range herself against a gate or a bank so that I could climb it and from there drop down into the saddle. This arrangement suited me fine, but it all collapsed when we went out hunting. Jenny went mad. She must, she thought, keep pace with all the loud-voiced people in exciting clothes who rode large and splendid hunters. Stop? Wait for the child to climb up again? Not bloody likely! Jenny had to keep up, scuttling through the heather as fast as her little legs would carry her. I learned quite quickly not to fall off and, if necessary, to hold on shamelessly to the saddle, something I was given to understand was 'simply not done'.

Hunting was exciting certainly, terrifying sometimes, but

early on I decided it was not for me. A quiet horse or pony to carry me was what I liked. I wanted to study the clouds, note how the thorn trees bend and twist in the wind, hear the buzzards screech. The moors have given me so much, and I have slipped little hints of my love into my novels.

## Animals and Birds

We never had many toys; children of my generation didn't. We had pets: dogs, rabbits, guinea pigs, perhaps a caged bird or a dormouse, if we were lucky a pony, and always on the strict condition that we looked after them ourselves carefully and

Thorn and bracken. These trees are red with berries in autumn and very attractive to birds.

*'Like some maize?' She stood looking down at Gus. 'Come on then.' Gus followed her while she fetched the maize. She threw a little on the grass. The gander ignored it. 'Gus, you must eat.' She sat down and the bird climbed onto her lap. 'Eat, you fool.' She held the bowl. Gus ate a little, pushing the corn about with his beak while she stroked him, pressing her hand along his back then curving it round his breast. 'You must keep up your strength for all those pretty ladies. You will like them, you know you will. You won't be lonely with them.' Gus got off her lap to stroll about cropping grass before coming back to stand behind her, leaning his neck over her shoulder, twisting it to peer up into her eyes.*

Jumping the Queue

properly. Caring for animals leads to affection as well as knowledge. This is probably why two or three times in my life a goose has become a pet or, as in the case of Gus in my novel *Jumping the Queue*, a devoted companion.

Geese are highly intelligent birds; to be called a goose should be taken as a compliment. Geese are, as the Romans knew, the best guards. At the sight of a stranger they will raise their heads and set up a loud chorus of honks, then lower their heads to ground level and approach the intruder hissing. Most people find this performance intimidating. They can also creep up on you from behind and, catching you unawares, painfully nip the calf of your leg, a useful deterrent for the uninvited guest. My geese, though, got to know me and would honk only in greeting. Geese are extremely affectionate birds. I kept geese during the war and we ate them, though the eating, delicious as it was, made me feel guilty for I had grown very fond of them; they were friends. I sympathized with my mother who also kept geese: when the day came for them to be killed she could not bear to stay at home but went off on a shopping spree to assuage her remorse and spent all her clothes coupons on quite unnecessary items for my father which he later refused to wear. In the event I compromised by eating only ganders, keeping the geese to lay eggs. Goose eggs make exquisite omelettes.

The loveliest geese I ever had were white Chinese. Six day-old chicks were sent to me by a breeder in Scotland. Their journey was delayed and took four days, yet when I opened their box they marched out in line quite unperturbed and at once started cropping grass. I was told by their breeder how to sex them: ganders had knobs on their beaks and geese did not.

As they grew up one gander became particularly tame and affectionate; we called him Pansy. He would sit on my lap, twine his neck around mine and peer into my face with his bright blue eye, making little throttling noises of affection. He, I decided, when the dread time came to kill the ganders, must

be spared; he was too gentle, too tame, too affectionate and would be no threat to the larger gander I was keeping.

A Toulouse goose.

A few days after the massacre I found Pansy sitting on a nest of winter-flowering heather; he had laid an egg. So much for the knob on the beak theory. Pansy became a family pet and laid many an egg, until, alas, like the fictional Gus, she fell foul of a fox.

# POLZEATH AND SOUTH SANDS
## *Early Childhood*

A sandy cove on the
Salcombe estuary.

*There was no wind; sea flat as a plate met sky the same colour as the water . . . The beach sloped so slowly to meet the sea it might have been an illusion that it inclined at all. Sand, dry as a biscuit near the shore, changed colour gradually, growing wetter, more sea-coloured as it smoothed close to the distant water.*

A Sensible Life

When I was taken to Cornwall by my mother in 1913, I was one year old. We went to Polzeath on the north coast, a very small place in those days. We travelled by train, my mother, my brother, my sister and our nanny. The object, I suppose, was 'sea air for the children'. My father was in the Army, so he and my mother were constantly separated (when we went to Cornwall he was probably on a posting in India), and on this occasion, like many others, we travelled without him.

This journey, the first I remember, was pretty straightforward. We got on the train at Paddington and left it in Cornwall, finishing the journey in a pony and trap. I suppose we stayed in Polzeath for several months. My first memories of the Cornwall I would grow to love are of vast stretches of sandy beach, high cliffs, and bumpy rocks I tried to climb – it was easier at that age to climb than to walk. I remember the deliciously salty taste of the clumps of bladderwrack seaweed I chewed. I listened to the sounds of gulls and sea, felt the sand between my toes and peered into rock pools. If a faulty memory serves, we went again to Polzeath some time during the 1914–18 war, for I can remember being older and standing on the seat in the train coming back to have my hair brushed by Nanny. I needed to be tidy on arrival at my grandparents' house in Montague Place, where we always stayed in London.

As I grew older the journeys became more complicated. There would be a French governess, the family dog, a dormouse in its cage and, on one occasion, thirty guinea pigs in a hamper. Instead of cuddly toys, children of my generation

With my brother and sister at Polzeath in 1913.

had live pets which we were taught to look after and feel responsible for. Where we went our pets came too.

This could be a problem when my mother decided to live for a while in France or Italy. Then the family dog had to visit long-suffering friends, but I still took my bullfinch in his cage. Totally wild when given to me, he grew to be completely tame and over the years he became a much-travelled bird who lived in London, Radnorshire, Italy, France and the New Forest. He attended boarding school with me in Sussex when my parents went to India and I was left behind, and he ended his life of captivity in Staffordshire one day when I let him out of his cage to snip the buds of Cox's orange pippins in my parents' garden. He met a hen bullfinch, decided not to return to his cage and flew off piping to live happily ever after. Many years later he appeared as the hero in my children's book *Speaking Terms*, a rather rude, arrogant, antibloodsport character.

## South Sands

Towards the end of the 1914–18 war, my mother rented a small house a couple of miles from Salcombe in a bay called South Sands. In those days there was our little house on the edge of the beach and the lifeboat shed, nothing else. A narrow lane ran along by the sea and over the hill to Salcombe; behind us rose the cliffs of Bolt Head from which there are wonderful views up the estuary and out to sea. Nowadays the cliffs belong to the National Trust and there are elegant signposts and strategically positioned lavatories. In 1918 we had them all to ourselves. Our beach was sandy and there were lots of shells; the rock pools were full of shrimps, crabs, sea anemones and a variety of seaweeds. The beach is barren now, the pools empty and, saddest of all, the smugglers' cave where we ventured heart in mouth is blocked up. Our house, solitary and small, has been swallowed up by a large hotel and the

Seashells on South Sands beach.

*She crouched by the water's edge and wrote in the sand, spelling out the names with her forefinger: Felix, Cosmo, Blanco. When I am seventeen, she had thought, I could marry Felix. He will be twenty-seven when I am twenty-two. But the sea rushed in, smoothing away the names, filling her shoes with frothy, sandy water. She had stood up and screamed into the wind, 'I shall, I shall, I shall.'*

A Sensible Life

28

South Sands and the Kingsbridge estuary.

boggy field of flag iris which ran down to the sea has become a car park.

In 1918 we had a dinghy from which we fished. In it my brother, aged ten, and two other little boys got swept out to sea on the tide but, catching hold of and clinging to a buoy, they managed to save themselves. I don't suppose my mother ever knew how close she came to losing her son, for he did not tell her and he told me only when he was an old man. 'We were amazingly lucky,' he said. 'We just clung on until the tide turned.'

From that dinghy I caught my first fish, a pollock. I vividly remember its disgusted expression as I pulled in my line.

My father appeared on leave from France, his hair clipped short for fear of lice. He was very quiet and, I later discovered, badly shell-shocked. Once he burst into song and it must have been very unusual or I would not have remembered it. He sang, 'Yip-yi-addy-yi-a-yi-a.' I think it was a music hall song.

We had a French governess whom my mother taught to swim. My older brother and sister swam well. I was cowardly, pretending I could swim and staying in the shallows. I did not learn until a year or two later when my sister pushed me off a pier in the Isle of Wight.

My mother was reading *Treasure Island* to us in the evenings and she would send me out of the room when she got to the frightening bits to spare my nerves. I have always associated South Sands with Blind Pew who handed out the 'black spot' which meant death, for, sitting on the stairs in the dark, I heard every word. I had nightmares for years afterwards. When I was about thirty I told my mother and she was extremely annoyed.

In the autumn of 1918 there was a tremendous gale and waves crashed and roared up to where our dinghy was supposedly safely beached. My sister and I watched our intrepid parent hurry to the rescue. It was night but there was a moon. I heard my mother shout, 'Come on, mademoiselle!' and the two women rushed into the sea in their dressing gowns, caught the boat and dragged it to safety.

*Flora along the cliff path to Bolt Head.*

It must have been one morning soon after this that the milkman driving his horse-drawn float called up to my mother, 'The Armytrice is signed, ma'm,' and my mother burst into tears. My father had survived.

Then the Navy brought a captured German submarine into the estuary. We rowed out to look and were allowed on board. There was no food on the ship, only some rotten potatoes. I felt very sorry for the Germans.

## Early Explorations

My mother never restricted our movements. My brother and sister and I wandered together or alone, covering what the modern child would consider quite long distances. We had liberty to fill our days as we chose, but we were expected to turn up in time for meals. The only warning I remember my mother giving me, for I often disappeared alone, was, 'If a strange man talks to you, darling, whip up your pony and canter on.'

Although I had learned to ride by the time she issued this injunction, I remember wondering what I should do if I were *not* on a pony. I was too shy to ask and all my childhood I went off by myself, not only in Devon and Cornwall but wherever we happened to be living in England or France or Italy. If a strange man had stopped me, I wouldn't have dreamed of telling my mother in case she restricted my movements. I don't think I was a particularly trustworthy child.

My generation was lucky; we grew up independent. We walked alone, rode alone, went to sea in boats and canoes alone, and wore

Once there was a smugglers' cave up there but now it is all blocked up.

32

RIGHT
The sea looking down
from the cliffs above
South Sands.

NEXT PAGE
View through trees in
winter of the estuary from
the coastal path.

no protective clothing, no life jackets or hard hats. If you fell off whatever you were riding, you dusted yourself down and got on again. If you fell out of the boat or canoe you swam. (To my astonishment, even dogs these days seem to wear life jackets.) I suppose our parents trusted us to be sensible, to develop an instinct for self-preservation and to discover that fear was something you had to learn to control.

I don't think my mother was a worrier and she did not have much imagination. One day she put us on a train which would take us to Dover and then across France to Italy where we were to stay with friends. We were all still very young; I was, I think, nine. My mother, perhaps having a sudden pang, shouted as the train began to move, 'Remember to get out at Camogli.' How we all laughed!

Some of the many varieties of flowers beside the coastal path.

As a small child I was
very frightened peering
over the edge of this cliff.
It was about here that our
dog would go rabbiting.

## My Father

From our house at South Sands we climbed a very steep hill which led to the cliff path to Bolt Head, a route which nowadays is clearly marked 'upper path' and 'lower path'. It was not so in 1918. We scrambled through furze and bracken and tripped into rabbit holes which were, of course, a delight for our dog.

One very hot day my sister and I were out with our dog when he plunged as usual down a rabbit hole, but this time he did not reappear, disappointed, to try the next one. What was worse, we did not hear distant yaps and growls. There was silence.

An hour or so later my father, on leave from the Front, came in search of his daughters and found them in a state of near hysteria. No dog. He must be lost, might have met a fox, was probably dead: total calamity. 'I will go back and fetch a pick and spade,' said my father. 'He may be stuck.'

We waited in agony until eventually my father returned, hot and tired, carrying a pick and spade. As he arrived our dog emerged from a hole and my father, seeing him, swore. I was deeply shocked. I had never seen my father angry with an animal (or anyone else for that matter). I had never heard him swear.

When he was old, in his eighties, I reminded him of this incident, for it had stuck in my mind. He said, 'Yes, I remember. I'm sorry, I was shell-shocked at the time, having blackouts.

The hotel at South Sands
as it is now. The small
house we lived in in 1918
has been incorporated
into the main building but
the lifeboat house
beyond is unchanged.

I was not in control. I was clinging to gates to keep upright, that sort of thing.'

I said, 'Did you tell Mummy?'

'Of course not,' he said, 'we could not tell our wives.'

Shortly after this he went back to the hell in France. He had already survived the whole of the Dardanelles and the battles of Mons and Ypres, losing all his friends. No wonder my mother wept with joy when the milkman told her the Armistice was signed.

Our dog, on the other hand, continued rabbiting as usual. When he was eventually run over by a taxi in Portsmouth, my father did all he could to comfort us.

## A Neighbour

When we lived at South Sands we walked to church every Sunday in Salcombe. Quite a hike, but we thought nothing of it. I remember little of the church services. We would, I suppose, since the war was still raging, have sung 'Eternal Father, strong to save' to cheer up the Navy wives and 'Onward, Christian soldiers, marching as to war' to give backbone to Army wives like my mother or perhaps the widows, of whom there were many.

What I do remember is a strange neighbour who owned and lived in the big house on the cliff. He would march down the lane alone, wearing a kilt and playing the bagpipes, a solitary eccentric. My mother never got to know this neighbour, so we never found out if what people said was true, that he was a German spy who flashed lights from his house perched high on the cliff, signalling messages to German submarines out at sea.

It was an agreeable, tingling, John Buchanish idea which gave a frisson of pleasure to the locals who invented it, but I for one, being a timid child, always hoped I would not meet the man on my solitary rambles. I never did.

*It must have been about here, Sophy thought, peering over. There was the ledge she had fallen on. If it had been anyone other than Monika one would think she had known she couldn't fall far. As she peered over, aware of the sea, the wind, the crying gulls, measuring the drop to the ledge, one of the many impertinent cliff foxes poor Ducks used to chase zigzagged along the slope.*

The Camomile Lawn

He was, come to think of it, a little bit scary – but not in the league of Blind Pew or Long John Silver, who really terrified me. They did not go to church; the bagpiper did.

## A Fortunate Age

As a child, I was fascinated by the flowers of south Devon in spring. I remember wondering where I could put my foot – not very large aged five or six – without treading on a primrose. Primroses carpeted the woods, the banks, the fields in a profusion which makes the primroses we still have seem sparse by comparison.

Snowdrops came first, then sweet-scented violets, then primroses followed by bluebells and later all the campions and cliff flowers. Orchids and iris grew in the valley and there was lots of ragged robin, now a rarity. All the hedges would be awash with may – and so on and on through the seasons.

There was no spraying of chemicals in 1918, just the spreading of honest dung from cow and horse. Attracted by the flowers and unharmed by pollution, quantities of butterflies and moths flourished. In the streams we found tadpoles which we kept in jars, releasing them into the wild when they turned into frogs.

We were, I believe, very fortunate children to live in an age when farming had not changed for a century.

The ferry for tourists is an innovation.
Chugging down the estuary from Salcombe,
it brings visitors to South Sands and the
National Trust cliff paths.

44

The coastal path from South Sands to Bolt Head.

When I was asked to list where I have lived in Devon and Cornwall, to explain Kim Sayer's lovely evocative photographs and suggest what part these places have played in my novels, I found it very difficult to point to any one place as being the location for a particular event, for I have mixed up the scenery in my mind to suit whatever I was writing. There is, for instance, the Terror Run in *The Camomile Lawn*. When writing this I remembered the coastguards' path which used to run – and probably still does – along the cliffs from Lamorna Cove to St Andellan and beyond, but I wrote as if it were far more perilous than it actually is. I can see it in my mind, and I hope readers can too, but should they go and look for it where *The Camomile Lawn* was filmed they will not find it, nor will they find the house I described in the book, a largish granite house with a broad lawn overlooking the sea.

When the film producers asked me where the house was I could only answer, 'It's in my mind.' In the event they found a house on a beautiful stretch of coast I had never seen before the film was made. The same goes for *Harnessing Peacocks* and *Jumping the Queue*: the locations they used were new to me.

When writing these books I remembered places I have lived in and loved, and described

The house used in the television series is a hotel. Visitors are still drawn to the location since the *The Camomile Lawn* was filmed there.

parts, but not all. For instance, in *Harnessing Peacocks* there is a cottage which, much to Kim's irritation, I simply cannot find. The old friend whose cottage it was gave me the silver spoon (see page 68). I described the cottage and how to reach it, but in the book I set it in a completely different location and now I can remember only where it is in the book. I cannot find my way

*The Camomile Lawn* was filmed here, on a stretch of exquisite National Trust cliff above Portloe. I had never seen either the cliffs or the house before the film was made.

*A torch flashed three times and Richard started his watch. They saw Oliver bound down the cliff, running hard along the narrow path which twisted through the bracken and heather, then close to the cliff edge past clumps of thrift and sea campion, through short grass which in spring was full of squills, past gorse still in flower, mixing its sweet smell with the heather.*

*Oliver ran feeling exhilarating fear. If he ran fast enough he would outstrip terror. He had never let the others know the extent of his fear of heights, of the vertigo which would paralyse him if he looked down. He ran a race against his weakness.*

The Camomile Lawn

A vision for the Terror Run.

back to reality, nor do I much want to. I like to remember the cottage as it was, very lonely and remote, swathed in mist. By now it has probably been tarted up, fitted out with all mod cons and completely transformed. Nor did my old friend remotely resemble old Bernard Quigley, the character in the book. He must have sprung, as some characters do, from passing remarks, some recollected gesture – a sniff perhaps?

I have never used South Sands, where I lived for two years as a child, specifically in a book. It may be that when I describe footprints in the sand or a stream ambling to the sea, I am drawing on my memories of those days.

Cornwall, on the other hand, I have used a lot. It is a very atmospheric county. I visited it as a child and constantly as I grew up, and I lived there for about seven years as an adult, first in the far south-west then in east Cornwall, not far from Lansallos. When writing *Jumping the Queue* I made the beach sandy, but my true recollection of it is that it was very stony and rocky, and there was no car park when we knew it.

From 1946 I lived for a long time on or on the edge of Dartmoor, so it inevitably colours my writing, but again there is no particular house or village, except perhaps Chagford. In my last book, *Part of the Furniture*, I mixed Devon and Cornwall, the sea and the moors, and called the house by a name I have read only on a signpost.

In 1981 I came to a halt where I live now, in the market town of Totnes. Apart from long periods in the south-west, my life has been peripatetic, but when I count the years on my fingers I find that I have lived longest in Cornwall and Devon. I used to think I was essentially a Londoner but perhaps I may call myself a country person after all.

## The Flower Farms

The Land's End peninsula has a mild climate which is suitable for flower farming. All along the cliffs and in the valleys, wherever

These cliffs, above Boskenna bay,
were good to climb.

Rocks off which we
swam at Boskenna bay.

there was shelter, there used to be flower fields, some as small as a squash court. Each field was protected by a low stone wall to keep out the wind, each plot planted by hand, weeded, dug and harvested by hand. When the flowers were harvested they would be loaded onto a horse-drawn cart and brought up to the flower sheds to be bunched and packed by the women and girls from the village, then loaded onto a lorry and sent off by train to London, Bristol or Birmingham.

Fifty years ago the flower industry gave work to a great many people. The season would start in late autumn with violets, anemones and polyanthus and end in April when the daffodils and narcissus were over. Romantic though it sounds, the work was backbreaking. Men and boys dug, planted and picked, the women bunched and packed; then, when the season was over, it was all to do again – weeding, digging, planting. The waist-high stone walls protecting the fields were all of course hand-built. In the war when I was living in Cornwall I helped with the harvest.

By Boskenna rocks with my children in 1944.

The flowers were grown in little fields running down the cliffs and valleys to the sea all along the coast from Lamorna to Land's End. Not long ago I came across King Alfred daffodils growing wild in Porthgwarra. It was the remains of a flower field gone back to nature, as have all the little fields I loved, for the traditional labour-intensive style of flower farming is no longer economic. Where local men bent their backs to dig and pick, the fields are now ploughed by tractors and harvested by casual labour. When I visit my old haunts I can still see the remnants of what were once neat stone walls, but the cliffs have taken back what is theirs; the daffodils and narcissus have given way to bracken and gorse.

*'Shall we go and see if we can snitch some of the General's violets?. . . Here we are. I shall sit while you pick a bunch.' Calypso sat on a rock and waved towards the violets planted in long rows. Obediently Brian picked, and as he picked he wondered how he could please this girl. The scent of wet violets roused his senses intolerably. Bending over the flowers he considered furiously how he could please her without getting himself court-martialled . . .*

The Camomile Lawn

55

Rounded and made smooth by the continual battering of the waves,
these rocks were fun to run across barefoot.

# Penberth

One of the most friendly and lovely valleys running down to the sea on the south-west coast of the Land's End peninsula ends in a small pebbled cove where fishermen haul up their boats and the trout stream which has ambled through the valley trickles its way to the open sea across the stones: this is Penberth. The Favell family who owned Penberth have given it to the National Trust in memory of Teddy Favell who was killed on D-Day, 6 June 1944, when he was still in his teens. His elder brother Richard was in submarines and survived the war.

The Favells were good landlords who did much for the area and though not Cornish – they originally came from up-country – were greatly loved by the inhabitants of Penberth and the parish generally, and accepted as honorary Cornish. There are, as anyone who has ever lived in that county knows, considerable differences between the Cornish and the English, and during the war, when I lived in Cornwall, the difference was a lot more obvious than it is now. Alice Favell was reminded of this difference and the Cornish suspicion of foreigners when, in 1940, with Hitler expected to invade at any minute, she was visited by two officers from the Royal Marine Commandos who asked whether they could inspect the cove and the cliffs for possible landing sites. Alice helpfully suggested that two of her fishermen should take them out in their boat so they could get a good view. The Commando officers accepted gratefully and when they returned she gave them tea and sent them on their way. Then she walked down to the cove to ask the fishermen how they had got on. 'Ah,' said the fishermen, 'we took them out. They was very curious, asked a lot of questions. We didn't tell them nothing.'

Nor was I ever told what had caused offence when Alice Favell, ill with flu, persuaded me to stand in for her at a ceremony involving the St Buryan Women's Institute. 'You just

*They were now tacking for home . . . The wind had increased and Julian yelled that they must shorten sail. Silas caught snatches of incomprehensible jargon and admired the boys as they nimbly obeyed. They looked serious now and Silas saw Julian look at the sky, frowning.*

*Clouds bulging with rain were surging in from the west. A black mass suddenly sheeted rods of water, as he remembered seeing in a Rembrandt print in a book of Hebe's.*

Harnessing Peacocks

Penberth fishermen.
The boats are
hauled up across
the stones.

stand up, say a few words and declare the sale open,' she instructed briskly. 'It's perfectly simple.' Somewhat reluctantly I did what I was told. I stood up, said a few words – I cannot remember what – and what happened? A message next day from the village: would I please never come again. I never discovered what I had said to give offence, but I was not Cornish and that was probably enough.

In 1940 there was one anti-aircraft gun for the whole of the Land's End peninsula, and this gun was positioned on the cliff above Lamorna Cove. Should it have to fire, we were told, it must move along the coast immediately afterwards so as to give the Germans the impression that we had lots of guns. When I wrote *The Camomile Lawn* I remembered this gun and the occasion when it was fired and the sorrow in the valley when it moved, the loss of custom for the pub, the loss of boyfriends for the village.

I do not suppose the German bombers who frequently flew along the coast at that period were much bothered by the gun. I was standing on the rocks one day with a group of evacuee children when a German plane flew overhead. One of them shouted, 'That's a Junkers 88 and it carries x number of guns!' The children waved and the pilot in his cockpit waved back,

Heading out to set lobster
pots off Penberth.

then flew on to drop a bomb on Coverack or Goonhilly Down.

Lamorna.

Once Alice Favell, walking on her cliff, watched fascinated as a bomber repeatedly dropped its load in the sea. When Richard telephoned his mother that evening she cried, 'Oh, I've had such an exciting afternoon watching a German submarine being bombed.' And Richard answered, 'Mother, that bomber was German, the submarine was me.'

Our defences were so weak that the Germans could fly along the coast in broad daylight. At night on their way back from bombing Bristol we would hear them droning over the house and sometimes they would drop their bombs in open country to lighten their loads. This went on until Beaufighters were stationed at Predannock to give chase. Then I would sit between my sleeping children's cots, just in case. One evening a bomb was dropped on Penzance and scored a direct hit on our wine merchant. I remember hearing it ten miles away as I lay in my bath. People said the gutters ran with claret and that the French fishermen scooped it up in buckets and basins, but this is a tall story. The French lived in Newlyn, down by the harbour. Nobody was hurt though there was structural damage. What we all mourned was the loss of wine. I used this incident, too, when I came to write *The Camomile Lawn*.

Chatting with an old friend in Penberth Cove.

# Merry Maidens

I lived for a while near the Merry Maidens, not far from St Buryan, and often rode among the stones. This part of Cornwall is too hilly for bicycling to be a pleasure, so I kept a pony instead of a bicycle and for fun we wove in and out of the Merry Maidens and trotted past the Drummer and the Piper who stand forever paralysed in Enoch Prouse's field on his farm, Boleigh. The pony would trot and canter and I would be carrying the shopping I had done in Penzance. The Merry Maidens are now of course heavily protected, not only from frivolous people like me but from tangle-haired young people of the New Age.

Long after the arrival of the Merry Maidens there came the Christians and they erected Boskenna Cross in the centre of the crossroads. It was just asking for cars to run into it and of course they did, so at some point the council in their wisdom moved the cross into the hedge and that makes me very angry, for it looks ridiculous and out of place, indicating nothing. It was naturally something of a hazard, especially during the war when we could use only sidelights on our cars, but I still think it wrong not to leave it where it was, to be a guide and comfort to travellers on foot or on horseback. Why should a scraped bumper matter compared to a holy cross that was there long before the automobile was invented? That cross was a sign of modernity when the Merry Maidens, the Drummer and the Piper were already ancient and rather sinister, certainly mysterious survivors from another age.

# Joe Boscence

I had a friend, a very old man, who lived in a tiny cottage near Sancreed; he had been an antique dealer all his life, working at Sotheby's or Christie's in London – I forget which – and eventually having his own shop in Chapel Street in Penzance. When I knew him best he had retired to this remote cottage filled

BELOW
The Drummer and the Piper stand in a field a quarter of a mile from the Merry Maidens. All the stones are now protected by the National Trust.

Among the Merry Maidens. According to legend, they danced on a Sunday and were turned to stone. The Drummer and the Piper ran off but did not get far.

with treasures in the middle of the Land's End peninsula. I used him and his cottage when I wrote *Harnessing Peacocks*, giving him a new persona. His name was Joe Boscence and he had the most prodigious memory for trivia; he would, for instance, tell me exactly what dress I had worn on an occasion I had long forgotten and what everyone else had worn and whether he liked it or the person wearing it.

The Merry Maidens.

Visiting him was something of an obstacle race for there was no road. I had to climb banks, thresh my way through fields of kale, and scramble over walls. 'If there was a road,' he said, 'people might use it. As it is, only people like you and Edwin John, who really love me, bother to come, and of course the postman.' I said, 'One day the postman will come and find you dead.' Joe Boscence agreed and that is indeed what happened, but not before he had played one or two tricks and with one of those tricks I am involved.

Joe Boscence owned a complete and beautiful set of Georgian silver: twelve forks and twelve spoons of every size. The set was entailed on a nephew, but he had once overheard the nephew's wife say to her husband, 'When the old man dies, we'll sell his silver.' Telling me this he became incensed. 'Look!' he exclaimed. 'Look, twelve of everything. Here, take this. I want you to have it. I will not let them have the complete set.' And he thrust into my hand a beautiful tablespoon and when I protested, he insisted.

I have the spoon to this day and every time I look at it I am reminded of my eccentric old friend. Occasionally I have a pang of conscience, easy to still, for I know how much satisfaction my friend derived from his righteous revenge. I value that spoon even more than a Worcester cup he gave me and a picture snatched from his wall. 'Here, darling, take this,' he said. 'I want you to have it.' Neither the cup nor the picture was entailed. The spoon is special.

Forty or fifty years later when I met the descendants of the inheriting nephew and his unwise wife – she must have had a carrying voice – I confessed to owning the spoon. Very generously they said yes, they knew the silver and were

The beautiful tablespoon given to me by Joe Boscence.

'We go across here.' Silas climbed a gate into a field.

'Isn't there a path?'

'No.'

Silas led the way through wet grass. Water seeped into their shoes, which squelched.

'We climb this.' Silas leapt at a bank and scrambled over it, dropping down into a field of kale. Giles followed. Silas trudged on, the tall kale brushing against his shoulders . . .

Giles . . . followed Silas to a clump of trees bent sideways by the prevailing south-wester. From the trees rose a drift of smoke. 'He's in.' Silas trotted to a wall and began to climb, putting his feet neatly between the stones. Giles followed. Silas called in his high child's voice:

'Mr Quigley, Mr Quigley, are you there?'

Harnessing Peacocks

A stretch of moorland near Sancreed on the
Land's End peninsula. Somewhere in this area my
old friend had his cottage.

*Giles looked round the room.
Chippendale chairs elbowed
Sheraton, occasional tables
overlapped one another, laden
with porcelain, silver, jade.
Every wall space was hung
with paintings and mirrors
which reflected the light from
the fire. There was barely room
for an oil lamp on the table near
the old man's chair. Several
candelabra stood on the floor,
messy with candle grease.
    Across the hall they could
hear Bernard moving about.
    'Do you think he likes snuff
or just wants to use his snuff
box?' Giles whispered, overawed.*

Harnessing Peacocks

aware that one lot of spoons was incomplete, but if that old
Boscence had given it to me, I must at all costs keep it. And so
that is what I have done.

## The Abbey Hotel

When Jean Shrimpton and her husband bought the old abbey
in Penzance and turned it into a hotel they furnished all the

Chapel Street in Penzance is a lovely street, charming, elegant and sedate. The Brontë family once lived there and the Abbey Hotel is in an alleyway off it.

rooms with antiques and covered the sofas and chairs with Colefax and Fowler chintz. Its atmosphere is not like that of any other hotel; guests feel that they are staying in a very pretty, very comfortable country house. The view from the windows is of Penzance harbour and Mounts Bay beyond with St Michael's Mount in the distance. Every bedroom has a bookcase which holds a wide choice of reading. For a truly lazy person there would be no need to go out at all because there are large open

The Abbey Hotel.

fires to sit and read by, really comfortable sofas and, should you look up from your book, a charming garden to enjoy.

From time to time I stay for a few blissful out-of-season days when I have breakfast in bed, stroll up Chapel Street visiting the antique shops, drive out into the country to see the haunts of my youth and then over to St Ives to visit the New Tate with its dazzling clear light shining in from the sea. I often think that should something really horrible happen in my life I would simply get into my car, drive down to Penzance, turn into the cobbled back yard of the Abbey Hotel, walk through the back door and instantly feel better.

ABOVE
Looking down towards
the harbour.

RIGHT
Gossiping with Jean
Shrimpton in the
drawing room.

Newlyn harbour.

A view of trawlers from
the quay, with the town
of Newlyn climbing
up the hill.

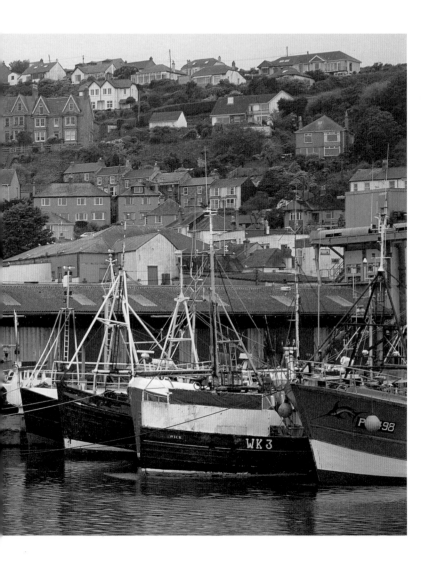

# Newlyn

At first glance Newlyn harbour today looks much as it did fifty years ago, though of course it has been modernized and improved since then. Newlyn is a long harbour sheltered by a sea wall. The inner harbour is crowded with trawlers with the distinguishing letters PZ (for Penzance) painted on their sides. Here you will find the busy fish market and the harbour office amid groups of cranes. On the western side of the harbour and pier lies Newlyn town: tightly packed houses and cottages, grey stone, slate roofs, narrow streets and alleys climbing up the steep hill. Newlyn faces east towards Penzance, Mounts Bay and the Lizard. A mile away around the corner sits the little port of Mousehole, famous for its lifeboat.

Newlyn was very busy when I first knew it, but these days the fishermen's lives are complicated by the European Union and catch quotas; there is an endless though necessary tangle of rules and laws that the fishermen find frustrating. But Newlyn harbour is ruled by a strong-minded lady called Elizabeth Stevenson who is the Harbour Master; she deals firmly and justly with fishermen and politicians, she speaks up on television, she fights the fishermen's cause and she makes sense.

I got to know Newlyn harbour during the war when it was

Sophy, home for the holidays, borrowed Mrs Penrose's bicycle to go to Newlyn harbour where, although entrance to the quays was forbidden to anyone without a pass, she had found that a blind eye was turned to a child, especially if the child brought eggs to barter for fish.

Sitting on an upturned lobster pot above a Belgian trawler tied to the quay, having swopped her eggs for a langouste, she listened to the fishermen talking with savage glee of the night's trawl in incomprehensible Flemish. Men drifted in twos and threes to join the group and slap backs, every now and then breaking into laughter.

The Camomile Lawn

From Newlyn looking east towards Mounts Bay.

ruled by Elizabeth Stevenson's great-uncle Brian. This robust, clever and amusing man spoke fluent Flemish, a talent which served him well. When the Germans invaded Belgium and France, the Flemish fishing fleet, disliking the prospect of a German occupation, packed their families, their possessions, their money, their cats, their dogs and in one case their priest and set sail, not pausing until they chugged into Newlyn harbour, a harbour they knew and had done business with for generations.

At the same time, inspired by similar motives, the Breton fleet set off from France and overnight the Penzance trawlers found themselves outnumbered by foreign friends. Cornish vessels rubbed hulls with Flemish and Breton, Newlyn harbour was cram-jam full and the Harbour Authority desperately busy – too busy, I happily noticed, to do anything about the strange

French crabbers
in Newlyn harbour
in the 1930s.

79

LEFT
Mackerel fishing boats
mooring at the market
early in the morning.

RIGHT
The catch is sold
at market early in the
morning and immediately
transported from
Penzance to all parts
of the country.

LEFT
Fishermen entering
Newlyn harbour, where
the fish are sorted
into boxes.

RIGHT AND ABOVE
The auction at the fish
market: prospective
buyers deliberate over
which boxes to buy.

83

A traditional box hook.

little dogs who hopped off their trawlers to lift a leg against Cornish bollards and exchange friendly sniffs with Newlyn dogs. (As far as I know nobody ever mentioned rabies or quarantine, there were so many other things to worry about; the foreign-looking little dogs melted into the landscape.)

Presently General de Gaulle or one of his minions, observing that the French and the Belgians were not overfond of each other, ordered the French fleet to move up the coast to spend the war in Brixham. Meanwhile the Cornish fishermen, many of whom were drafted into the Navy and Merchant Navy, had perforce to leave the fishing to the Belgians who effectively occupied the harbour. For the duration of the war, the Belgian children went to school with the Newlyn children and they keep in touch and visit one another to this day. As the friend I lived with and I both spoke French, one of our WVS jobs was to offer help to Belgian wives. My friend came home much amused after visiting a Belgian wife to enquire whether she was managing all right with the rations. 'She said,' my friend told me, 'that she had been up to London to have a look round and had found a very reasonable grocer called Fortnum and Mason.'

Newlyn harbour was closed to visitors. Motor torpedo boats came and went on mysterious missions, odd-looking craft jostled among the trawlers; one did not ask questions. Practically all the fish was loaded directly onto the train and sent up-country to London, Birmingham and other large cities. It was possible, however, if one was a friend of Brian Stevenson, to visit his office and swap eggs, vegetables and flowers for crayfish, lobster or Dover sole and listen to Brian's intelligent and funny conversation. I wonder now what he would make of the European Union regulations and quotas and enough red tape to tie up a whale. Certainly he would be proud of his great-niece Elizabeth; he too would have fought for the Newlyn fishermen and run rings round visiting politicians.

A tired old trawler
at low tide.

## Cliffs at Land's End

Cliffs are made for climbing. Nobody when I was young wore a protective helmet or special shoes. We would have thought such things rather ridiculous. I climbed, I seem to remember, as often as not barefoot or in socks, scrambling up as far as possible above the sea to peer down into its depths. One wonderful morning I looked down from my high perch on a school of basking sharks weaving slowly through the water, sifting plankton, huge creatures both ungainly and graceful.

I enjoyed exploring the cliffs alone but one day a friend said he would come too; he did not tell me he was afraid of heights. Suddenly he was stuck, unable to move, completely paralysed. I was very angry and had quite a job to get him down, guiding his reluctant feet and cursing him for not having warned me of his vertigo. Fortunately my anger had a galvanizing effect and I felt no fear for him until much later when I was ready to be sympathetic. I knew my own father was terrified of heights, though sensibly he did not pass on his fear to his children. So I climbed the cliffs at Land's End for pleasure; they are lovely to climb, quite unlike the cliffs on the Lizard which crumble and are very dangerous. A friend and I once fell asleep in a cove on the Lizard, the tide came in and there was nothing for it but to climb. As we climbed – both of us unsuitably shod – the cliffs gave way underfoot, handholds were insecure and I realize now we were lucky to reach the top, lucky not to slip and fall.

From these cliffs we saw the *Torrey Canyon* when it sank in March 1967 spilling all its oil.

I am now too old to climb but not too old to remember the exhilaration of scrambling high, then looking down at the waves below sucking at the rocks, unable to reach up to us, the water dragging and pulling even on calm days when the sea was deep and clear. I remember also the excitement of winter storms as immense waves roared and crashed against the rocks, sending up spume to make one's hair sticky with salt. What, one wondered, if one lost one's footing? Would death come quickly?

In my day Land's End was unspoilt by the theme park which now wrecks its beauty. Then there were only the huge cliffs, the howling gales and roaring waves; one could just see the Scillies crouching in the distance, then nothing until America. I fantasize about being very, very rich, buying up the theme park, clearing it all away and letting Land's End get back to what it once was: beautiful, savage, dramatic, wild.

## Peakswater near Lansallos

With my son Toby, who is on the pony I rode instead of a bicycle.

In 1947 when we bought Peakswater, we thought, my husband and I, that we would be settled for ever in this delightful little house writing our novels and living a peaceful, productive country life. We had not been able to find a house we could afford in Chagford where we had really wanted to live, but Peakswater – which had been, I believe, a country pub in the eighteenth century – seemed perfect.

It stood facing a lane by a bridge. There was a trout stream for a boundary, a large orchard behind the house and several good-sized fields. It seemed pretty good to us. True, there was

The path down to Lansallos Cove.

no electricity; we bought Tilley lamps and candles. We had no water except from a spring; we installed a pump and built a bathroom. The cooker was one of those black iron Victorian jobs you pay the earth for nowadays in junk shops; we put in a Rayburn.

There was no telephone and we had no car, but all the tradesmen came in vans. There were good shops in Lostwithiel and Fowey; we had strong legs and could walk and we shared a bicycle. The sea at Lansallos was within easy walking distance.

Eric settled down with his typewriter to write a novel. I set about redecorating the house, stripping layer after layer of paper off the walls, each layer older and prettier than the last, until finally I had painted and distempered it throughout.

I retrieved the old pony I had had in Cornwall during the war from where he had been lodging with my sister, and a friend gave me a very old but sprightly Welsh pony who had once won the jumping at Olympia, and for good measure a large unbroken cob. What she did not tell me was that the Welsh pony was a wanderer who jumped or barged her way out of the stoutest-hedged field, or that the cob still had one testicle and was to all intents and purposes a stallion. I spent many hours that year retrieving my horseflesh in answer to messages saying, 'Your horses are in my corn,' or 'I can't be doing with that cob, he goes for me.' The cob, whose name was Joe, did indeed rush at strangers, ears back and teeth snapping. Strangers were not to know that he responded and followed like a Pekinese if you said, 'Come off it, Joe, stop that nonsense. It's time to go home.'

In addition to this horseflesh I bought two piglets. As food was still rationed, ham and sides of bacon made sense. Unfortunately, before they were old enough to become ham, the pigs became friends who accompanied us for walks, answered to their names, Bentham and Hooker, and considered themselves part of the family. When eventually we ate them it was without joy. 'Is this Bentham or Hooker?' a child would ask

From this cove in my novel *Jumping the Queue* Matilda swims out to drown. It is a stony cove but in the book I made it sandy and much longer.

Gull at Land's End.

sadly, laying down his knife and fork. Still on the track of self-sufficiency, I acquired a broody hen and sat her on three goose eggs which, when they hatched, grew to be partly the originals of Gus in *Jumping the Queue*. The other part was inspired by a Chinese goose I had years later at Thornworthy. Long after the geese hatched and became independent their foster mother paid for her keep by laying an egg every day. Eventually I found her a good home.

All seemed set for an idyllic if fairly strenuous existence. We were happy. We woke in the mornings almost deafened by the dawn chorus. Thrush, blackbird, robin, tit and warblers – I have never heard better.

Eric worked on his novel, I tinkered with mine. We went for enormous walks inland and by the sea, and watched a spring of unrivalled beauty. I have never seen such wildflowers, a mass of daffodils and primrose and later fields of orchids. The children arrived for their school holidays, rode and roamed the countryside, and we all swam at Lansallos. Gradually, since no publisher had evinced any interest, we ran out of money. Eric was offered a job as the *Sunday Times* correspondent in Berlin so off he went to Germany and soon I joined him there. From a distance we sold the house; it had been a good try.

Many years later, a friend wanted to see Peakswater. I had forgotten the way, had trouble finding it and when I did, I wished I hadn't. It had become a caravan site. Caravans stood in rows where my pigs had wandered, where my ponies had grazed. The stream looked sullen and even the ghost of Gus – a gander who had never existed except in my mind – failed to show. The fields which I had seen pink with orchids had been ploughed and sprayed, and few birds sang.

When I wrote *Jumping the Queue* I thought of Peakswater and Lansallos but, as one always does, I mixed them in my mind with the cottage I was then living in on the edge of Dartmoor, and I added an almost entirely imaginary beach.

*The wind had dropped, the sea was subsiding. Between the islands the water was pewter-coloured in the evening light, smoothing itself calm. He watched the sunset begin its spectacular. Yellow light seeping under storm clouds gave the impression that golden treacle had been spread over the sea between the islands. As he watched the colours changed from gold to pink. The heather at his feet was spun with spiders' webs, raindrops reflecting the reddish purple of the heather and occasional blue of Devil's Bit. There was no sound other than the soughing of the wind, gulls and the sea pounding on the rocks.*

Harnessing Peacocks

Rocks at Land's End
with the Scilly Isles in
the distance.

*The Wild Moor*

For me the apparent emptiness of Dartmoor is probably its principal attraction. High on the hills with the moor stretching away as far as the eye can see, it is possible to be truly alone. A day walking or riding on the moor and not meeting another human being is my idea of bliss.

A great number of visitors come to Dartmoor, especially in summer. Dartmoor is after all a national park, a place to picnic, paddle in streams, fly kites, perhaps swim in the rivers, feed the ponies. (Feeding the ponies is strictly illegal but tourists continue to do it.) So how does somebody like me contrive to be alone?

With our dog
Pebble and Toby.

Fortunately, at selected places on the moor, near sites of particular beauty or interest, there are large car parks, almost always with an ice-cream van and probably a WC. This is where the visitors congregate. The average visitor does not like going far from his car; indeed quite a lot of visitors do not leave their cars. They sit and look at the view and read the paper while their children fly kites, play football and eat ice-cream. They do not leave the road or if they do they keep in sight of their car, for they have read a police notice warning them that a lot of cars get stolen.

I do leave the road and, like other moor lovers, set off across country where it is possible to walk or ride all day without encountering another human being, and this I love. One of my sons managed recently to walk for four hours without sighting another soul, and this was in the middle of August.

When we first came to Chagford, my husband and I used to walk the moor with our dogs until we were so exhausted we would drop down from the heights into the nearest village and

*'Where have you been?'*

*'For a walk.'* *She had no intention of sharing the joy of her walk. The tramp across fields and moorland, the sound of water dripping from trees, the rustle of wind, cries of sheep, shriek of buzzards, the delicious solitude.*

*'I would have come with you if you'd said.'*

*I dare say you would, thought Hebe, climbing the stairs without answering.*

Harnessing Peacocks

A typical Dartmoor stone wall and
beech trees shaped by the wind.

*Flora listened as she rode to the bits jingling, the creak of leather, the brush-brush of the horses' hooves through the grass, the croak of a carrion crow in the valley. As the sun rose and the wind stroking the yellow grasses dropped, they reined in their horses, let them crop the turf and sat watching the view.*

A Sensible Life

Standing stones which have been used as gateposts in the remains of a stone circle.

get a taxi home. On those expeditions we saw neither hide nor hair of another person. Gosh, we were happy.

I find peace on the moor. Dartmoor has consoled my grief, comforted loneliness, understood happiness and elation. I probably love it best in winter when the heather, nipped by the frost, looks almost black and the bracken a golden brown. It is very lovely too in snow.

I love the thorn trees bent and twisted by the gales or, as in sheltered valleys, swathed in greenish-grey lichen. I love the deep wooded valleys where the rivers run and the ravens fly croaking overhead. I love the cry of the buzzard, the moor pony's neigh, the call of ewe to lamb. This solitude calms and relaxes me so that I can hear the faint rustle of an adder as it slithers off the stone where I have disturbed it sunning itself.

When I think of this magical tract of land, I remember how my husband's family, as children, were caught by the vicar as they tried to escape into the country when they should have been in church. He did not reproach them but grinned and said, 'Ah, Bluedomers, I see.' Perhaps Dartmoor has made me into a Bluedomer.

## A Startling Encounter

I first discovered Dartmoor during the war. A friend and I, together with our small children, found a farm at Haytor which had comfortable rooms, was two minutes from the moor, five from the pub and had good horses to ride. The moor was empty except for its few inhabitants and a sprinkling of soldiers in training; it was possible to ride for miles hearing nothing but the swish of our horses' feet through the heather and larks singing. The war seemed a very long way off.

Later we would repair to the pub which in those days was very small and owned by an eccentric character who was said to be a retired stockbroker. He had stocked up all right. Behind

the bar in those times of shortage his shelves were stacked with whisky, gin, vodka and brandy in all their varieties and, should he like the look of you, the landlord would serve you a drink, just one, but should he not like the look of you, you got cider. Fortunately for us we both passed muster. Often we were treated to the spectacle of strangers coming into the bar and gasping in astonishment at the rows of bottles so bravely displayed. Realizing that what they saw was not a mirage, they would order a double vodka, whisky or gin. Having sized up the strangers the landlord would often reply, 'Nothing but cider,' and that was what they got. Fifty years on I still refer to that inn as the Nothing but Cider Pub. The bar shelves remained glorious but the drinks were rationed until the war ended and supplies flowed again.

The colours and textures around Haytor
in the evening light.

Once I had discovered Haytor I went back quite often and on one occasion, having had an operation in London, I went to recuperate. I had first asked my surgeon whether I could ride. 'As long as you don't let your horse go out of a walk,' he said. 'Be careful.' A friend came to see me and suggested he come riding too. He ran the Cornish Home Guard and was hoping to create a Mounted Home Guard for Bodmin Moor and Dartmoor. (In that way he would get rationed corn for his hunters; he was, I should explain, a hunting man, quite a reckless rider and a considerable drinker.) I told him that because of my recent operation the ride must be sedate.

We walked our horses across the moor, chatting as we went, until somewhere beyond Hound Tor we came to a gate into a field and rounding the corner encountered a large herd of llamas.

Bunching together, the llamas advanced on us, ears laid back, spitting. Our horses were terrified. They reared up, swung round and bolted. Weak from my operation, I was whirled away at a gallop and as I went I saw my bibulous friend had gone ashen white.

'It's all right, I've seen them too,' I shouted.

'Thank God for that!' he called after me. 'I thought I'd got the DTs at last.'

The gallop did me no harm and back at the pub my friend was served with a recuperative double. The llamas, we later discovered, had been evacuated from Paignton Zoo after being frightened by bombs dropped on Torbay. Years later, when I was writing *The Camomile Lawn*, I remembered this incident and used it to give Polly concussion and rearrange her love life.

## Favourite Walks

I do not pretend to know the whole of Dartmoor well. There are still parts of the moor I have never been to but the parts I do know I know very well, for when we lived at Chagford we were great walkers. One walk we constantly made was up onto

*'I walked,' said Polly in recollection . . . 'Then I hired a horse and rode. I could get further into the moor. I rode right across there.' Polly pointed. 'I picked my way round that very rocky tor and not terribly far on the other side there was a moorland farm, green fields fenced in by stone walls around the top of a valley with a stream at the bottom. Emerald fields, blue sky, larks singing, I particularly remember the larks. Then suddenly round a corner came a herd of llamas, white against the sky. My horse reared up terrified, the llamas spat, the horse bolted, I lost my stirrups, the horse jinxed, I fell off.'*

The Camomile Lawn

Meldon Hill above Chagford, from the top of which you can see for miles across the moor and over towards the Bristol Channel. The climb was steep and, gasping for breath, we would sit on a rock at the top of the hill and gaze at the comforting view of fields and moorland stretching to infinity. Our dogs too loved Meldon for there are rabbits, foxes and badgers and our dogs were devilish hunters, disappearing into the bracken and down a hole to scrabble and dig, deaf to all our whistles and shouts. Years later, when we were living at Thornworthy, they would sneak off and vanish, only to be found many hours later after a long search, their paws sore from digging, their eyes bunged up with grit, happy and unrepentant. In fact their hunting became so excessive we were reduced to letting only one dog out at a time – they hunted in couples – and should two be out by mistake there would be a cry of 'Dogs out!' and I would rush to the telephone and alert the farmers across whose land they would pass. 'Mr So-and-So, our dogs are out and they will be running through your fields. They do not chase sheep.' The farmer would answer, 'That's all right, missus, I know they do no harm. You'll find 'em on Meldon.'

Another part of the moor I know well – indeed the first part I ever knew – was round Haytor, where I rode when I first discovered the then empty moorland. The Tor is the highest point on Dartmoor. It is now a honeypot for trippers and the paths have grown wide from the many feet which tread them. I do not stop at Haytor these days. I drive on to find a more solitary, less accessible part.

We had no car and other walks we regularly made when first living in Chagford were along the river Teign, following the stream up the valley by the fishermen's path beside the water. As we walked we talked of our books yet to be written and what we were reading at the time, or more often we walked in silence watching the water flow, chuckling, peaty yet clear. There were fish to watch in those days; it was before the

*What she saw was a stretch of moor etched starkly by the moonlight above a wooded valley. To the left of the woods lay a pattern of silvery fields round a group of stone buildings. Barns? A farm? A glint of water zigzagged through the fields to a large pond, to reappear wider and swifter on its way through the woods, to a valley, to the sea, perhaps? It was difficult to judge distances. As it cut through the fields she felt a longing to follow.*

Part of the Furniture

RIGHT
Stepping stones across the Dart at Huccaby, a favourite place for a swim.

106

TOP The moor above Holne in winter.
BELOW Winter near Fernworthy.

ABOVE Ponsworthy.
BELOW Remains of a Stone Age hut.

disastrous decline of the salmon. On one incredible occasion, after a long period without rain we saw salmon waiting in a pool to move upriver to spawn, so many and so tightly packed we felt we could have walked across the river on their backs. Now, alas, more than forty years on, you are very fortunate to see a fish at all, for salmon farming, overfishing and pollution have depleted the stock of wild salmon to a dangerous degree.

Another regular walk we made was downriver from Easton Court, past the salmon pool which lies below Castle Drogo and down along the river gorge which runs through woods. Beautiful at any time of year, the gorge is unique for the moor; solitary in our day, it is now signposted and discovered by walkers. There is also a parallel path high up from which the view is remarkable. The salmon pool has happy memories for me. Our dogs swam in it and it was there that the local post-man taught my young son to cast a fly. There was a footbridge and, as often as not, a kingfisher.

This pool at Huccaby is where, when we lived on the south side of the moor at Cullaford Cottage, I would take my grand-children to picnic and swim. There are stepping stones and shallow pools and deeper ones. The children loved hopping across the stones and bathing and making dams which would be swept away with the next rain. In that valley too there are many thorn trees draped with lichen. I have not used any of these places in my novels but they have of course influenced my thinking.

When I wrote my second children's book, *The Sixth Seal*, I was living at Cullaford and thinking of Thornworthy, in particular the moor between Thornworthy and Buckfast; also the river Dart and the moor stretching between Chagford and Plymouth. I changed the locations around to suit. In the book there is a monstrous storm which blows people away and fells trees. When writing the book I had seen one of our enormous beeches at Cullaford suddenly heel over and fall,

Winter landscape above Spitchwick.

110

A wall near Holne. All over the moor these medieval walls divide the land and mark the roads.

an extraordinary sight. I described in the book a beech tree I used to see from my bedroom window at Thornworthy blown down, and in the writing it seemed very real to me – so much so that when I took Kim Sayer to see Thornworthy and went up to the room that used to be my bedroom, I was amazed when I looked out of the window and there was the tree still standing! Kim Sayer photographed me looking out of

ABOVE
The damp river valleys provide a perfect climate for mosses and lichen.

RIGHT
The river Dart is swollen in winter with water pouring down from Dartmoor.

112

the window, staring at the beech tree blown down but not
blown down. Blowing it down in print, I had believed it gone.
My writing, in which I have used or invented trees or houses
or places, has distorted my knowledge of Dartmoor.

When we lived at Thornworthy there was a gate when you
got to the moor. Now, as in many other places, there is a cattle
grid. I used the moor gate when I wrote *Part of the Furniture*.
Robert struggles with it in the wind and the snow when he
comes back from London and his son's funeral. In the book the
gate is not on Dartmoor but in an imaginary location near the
sea and only in part resembles that particular gate, that bit of

The character of
Dartmoor changes so
quickly. Dramatic skies
signify a change from
clear weather to low
cloud and poor visibility.

moor. Yet the cattle grid is there and rattles when you drive over it.

I know the moor well enough not to get lost when riding. I have several times set off in fine weather and suddenly become enveloped in fog which has made me completely disorientated and curiously deafened, all sense of direction gone. The trick on these occasions is to drop your reins on the horse's neck and leave it to the horse. Your horse will prick up its ears, swing round, take off in what may seem to you quite the wrong way and if you leave well alone will carry you home. The horse or pony knows best.

If you are planning a ride on the moor, it is a good idea to find an animal which has some Dartmoor pony in its blood. Those animals know how to manage in a bog. They know instinctively how to pick their way from tussock to tussock and not sink in.

I know and love villages such as Manaton. I greatly appreciate Widecombe in winter when it is relatively free of trippers. I dearly love Buckland in the Moor with its tiny church with the clock face that says 'To my dear Mother'. No, I would not make a reliable guide, for my Dartmoor is too much a mix of the real, the imaginary and the unknown.

The footbridge across
the top end of the
salmon pool below
Castle Drogo.

# The Easton Court Hotel

We used the Easton Court Hotel near Chagford as our base and lived there for months at a time in 1949–50 when Eric was changing jobs or we were house-hunting.

The hotel had been opened just before the war by an American called Carolyn Cobb and her partner Norman Webb. Their idea was to create a refuge where writers could work in peace without the interruptions of housekeeping and family. They bought a thatched house on a crossroads a mile or so out of Chagford, within sight of Castle Drogo and half a mile from the river Teign. They added a wing and some bathrooms, installed central heating, comfortable beds, and in every room a solid table fit for a typewriter. Dogs were welcome.

Carolyn made it clear that writers would be the most acceptable form of guest, though ordinary people were welcome too. Wisely, she forbore to install a bar. Should guests feel in need of a drink, they must walk a mile to Sandy Park or into Chagford. The word was spread, writers came: Evelyn and Alec Waugh, Lord Snow, Patrick Kinross, Michael Polanyi and many more including Eric and me with our dogs and, in the holidays, the children. By the time Eric and I took to coming, Carolyn was ill and lived separately from the hotel in an annex. She did not necessarily like all her guests and in later years she spoke only to those she did like. We would visit her for a gossip and wonder when and whether we would be able to pay our bills, though once when I mentioned this delicate subject it was brusquely brushed aside: 'You can pay your bill when you get an advance from your publisher.' She would have had to wait until long after she was dead in my case, and fortunately she did not have to do so.

Carolyn was incredibly kind. When I got mumps and had to stay in bed for a month, no fuss was made, meals were ferried up on trays and armfuls of crime novels supplied. Crime novels were Carolyn's weakness. It was she, too, when we were house-hunting

The river Teign near the Easton Court Hotel. The river runs through a wooded valley for several miles, with a fishermen's path alongside.

*He parked his car, tucking it into the side of the road, pulled on his gumboots and, standing in the quiet of the August evening, put up his rod. Choosing a fly from his flybox, he listened to the gurgle of water flowing under the bridge and the evening sounds, the imagined rustle of bats hunting over the water, the rhythmic chewing from a group of recumbent cows who watched him benignly as he climbed a stile and began his slow progress along the river, casting his line over the water with the flick of wrist and movement of arm of inborn talent. As he cast his line he cast his cares. The mesmeric flow of the water brought solace and comfort to his insecure soul. When a trout rose to the fly and he struck, excitement took over until he had landed it, killed it with a sharp knock on the head and put it in his bag.*

Harnessing Peacocks

for the second time, who suggested we look at Thornworthy which was to let. We went, we looked, we rented.

Not surprisingly the hotel (affectionately known to aficionados as the Cobbwebb) did not run at a profit but, thanks to Carolyn's personal fortune and the force of her personality, it kept going until she died. At Carolyn's funeral a clutch of writers mingled with the crowd. She would have enjoyed the sight of Evelyn Waugh and my husband exchanging glances across her open grave. They had disliked each other for many years, ever since they were at Oxford together.

The Cobbwebb is still a hotel. In other hands, it is much changed but the spirit of the place and the generosity of its creator are not forgotten.

ABOVE With my husband Eric, Roger and Toby.

RIGHT The Easton Court Hotel as it is today.
When we knew it, it was not covered in ivy.

The river Teign below Chagford.

124

FAR LEFT
High Street in Chagford.

LEFT
Bowden's, 'the shop
which stocks everything'.

# Chagford

When we first discovered Chagford in 1948 it was a much smaller place than it is now. House-hunting, we stayed in a guest house run by a delightful couple who welcomed us and our dogs and my two schoolboy sons in their holidays. They had two children of their own, one of whom grew up to marry an Aussie called Rolf Harris. Eric and I were both writing novels – neither got published – and after work we walked across a valley we called 'the bog' and climbed up Meldon Hill, where our dogs hunted rabbit, fox and badger while we sat catching our breath and gazed at the glorious view across the moor. The bog has now been built over – rows and rows of modern houses with driveways and neat gardens – but Meldon Hill, thank God, remains the same. On other days we followed the river Teign upstream and watched the salmon, and one strange autumn day we walked through a rainbow.

Chagford, then as now, boasted many pubs. The one we favoured was the Three Crowns, ancient, granite-built, thatched. The landlord was a former sergeant of the Guards who disapproved of women in pubs; settle seats lined the walls, sawdust lay on the floor and plenty of rough cider was consumed. Dogs were welcome and talk was of a military nature, male dominated. When the ex-Guardsman retired, the pub changed; carriage lights proliferated amid the red plush, women were welcome, dogs were not, and cider seemed to vanish from the bar in favour of more sophisticated drinks. There was soft muzak. We changed pubs.

Enjoying a pint in the Chagford sunshine.

Chagford church.

The lane leading from the
farmyard at Thornworthy
onto the moor.

Now when I go to Chagford I am amazed by the number of
posh cars and Land-Rovers which have replaced the vans and
jeeps and farmers' tractors I knew. Parking, once so simple, has
become an art. As Chagford has grown, nearly all the shops
have changed. Gone is the fascinating junk shop where, among
layers of cracked crockery and glass, one could discover dusty
Minton or Chelsea; the antique shops are now as sophisticated
and expensive as anywhere else. Only Bowden's remains. Famous

126

Thornworthy from across the fields.

for its immense variety of stock, it is still run by the Smith family, although the Smiths who inherited from their father are no longer little boys but grandfathers. Later, when we lived at Thornworthy, we went to mass in the village hall, sniffing as we received the host great whiffs of stale tobacco and beer left over from some meeting of the night before, especially pungent if the meeting had been held by the British Legion. When I told the Jesuit priest who had received us into

the church he greatly approved; he had been a chaplain in the 1914–18 war.

Our barber, however, did not approve; he thought we should have a proper church and to rectify the situation he started a lottery. The lottery caused a certain amount of shock in the village. Some thought it unfitting, rather raffish, the sort of thing 'those Catholics' would do, but quite a number of collectors for good causes wished they had had the idea first. Tickets were, I think, sixpence or a shilling and I of all people won the first prize, a lordly five pounds. After that lots of people bought a weekly ticket and today at the lower end of the village in a discreet cul-de-sac, well out of sight of the lovely parish church which dominates Chagford, stands a neat little Catholic church. I wonder whether anyone remembers the lottery?

So Chagford as we first knew it remains the same only in its heart. The square, the church and the pubs have not changed nor ever will, and all the new buildings will grow old too. The green fields are built over, but I can still stand in the square and remember my son's wedding in the lovely church, the funerals of friends, and the Easter flowers. I recognize the clang as I open the great door to step inside, then walk through the churchyard into the square where, though much has changed, the real people have remained the same. Others come down from London and buy a house, then presently they sell and move elsewhere, while the generations of people born and bred in the area stay on. The farmers and foresters remain as they were in the Civil War, when Chagford stood for the King and its neighbour Moretonhampstead for Cromwell, though nobody in either village can really remember why to this day the two villages distrust each other.

ABOVE
Looking out from what had been my bedroom window at Thornworthy. To my surprise, the beech tree I had blown down in a novel was still standing.

RIGHT
Winter can be bitter for the animals.

# Thornworthy

For us, the charm of Thornworthy was that the house is at the end of a lane which leads up to the hills above Chagford and, reaching Thornworthy, stops. The house, the farm, the lodge and the cottage all stand well apart. From the yard and the garden there is nothing but the moor on which we walked or rode for mile upon mile of glorious country. We were very high up there and had wonderful views. The farm was run by Harold Wonnacott and his wife. The cottage (so-called) was inhabited by our landlady and the lodge by the gardener we shared with her. Our nearest neighbour was a farm a mile down the hill. There were farmyard noises by day – cattle, horses, sheep, no cars – and by night the sound of the wind and owls.

The house was far too large for us and difficult to run. It had its own water supply, an electricity generator which was for-ever going wrong or catching fire and a central heating system which may well have been among the first in England. Jackdaws built their nests in the chimneys. Thornworthy was a house of character. We loved it. Two of my sons were still at school when we arrived and my youngest was one. School and university friends were not long in discovering we had a lot of spare beds and our youngest child had the privilege of starting

Ponies above
Thornworthy. Hay will
be brought to them
on a tractor.

The lane to Fernworthy in summer and winter.

The valley of Widecombe.

life in a place where he could wander at will in safety. We were half a mile from Fernworthy reservoir where we had a boat for fishing. It is a bird sanctuary now and there are no boats and the house has been modernized out of all recognition. There are no dramas when the generator explodes, and draughts have been eliminated by double glazing. There is up-to-date central heating. The back stairs, the walk-in larder and the butler's pantry have

disappeared. There are many excellent bathrooms where once there was only one. After an interval in which it became an hotel, the house is now once more a private home.

One had to cross a stretch of moor to reach Thornworthy. In our day the moor gate caused many a tussle in high winds. I used memories of that gate and much of the house in *Part of the Furniture*.

I kept white Chinese geese at Thornworthy – and lots of chickens. We woke in the mornings to the sound of cockerels and gaggling, the baas of sheep and a pony neighing. In summer we rode over the moor to a stretch of the upper Teign, which we dammed as a swimming pool. There were otters in the lower Teign below the house who teased our dogs. I wonder whether they are still there or long gone?

Supplies came from Chagford, a drive downhill through narrow lanes. Even in our day the village had everything we needed. There was no necessity to venture as far as Exeter. Our nearest railway station, long closed, was Moretonhampstead. In winter, when we were snowed in, shopping could become quite complex. There were no four-wheel drives in those days, no Land-Rovers, but I could telephone the baker or butcher or they would ring up. 'I have put your shopping on Mr X's tractor,' they would say. 'He will get it as far as Thorn.' From Thorn, another tractor would take over and eventually we would meet it at the moor gate with a sled.

*Juno murmured, 'Smells,' aware that scent, beginning with the first primrose, had contributed much to her happiness in recent months — grass after rain, freshly tilled earth between rows of vegetables, the sharp tang of box, the stuffy smell of hen where an obstinate fowl laid a daily egg in Millicent's manger, horse shit, cowpats, the stink of fox in the wood, cows' breath, the warm smell of pig, the tang of sheep, the crazy mix of lilac, roses, honeysuckle and wisteria which drifted in at her window as the wall of the house cooled, the secret whiff of bluebells under the beeches in the wood, the sharp tang of freshly chopped logs and the salt breeze on the cliff where she had sat with Robert . . .*

Part of the Furniture

When I wrote *The Sixth Seal* I thought of Thornworthy in the snow, and in *Jumping the Queue* I remembered my geese. One year we were thoroughly cut off. Snow was two feet deep outside our door and, looking out, I saw a soldier staggering about in the yard. He turned out to be one of a company who had been sent out on a short exercise in fine weather. Caught by sudden snow, they had become disorientated and lost. The rest of the company had taken refuge in a ruined farm across the moor and refused to move.

The maps the Army were given in those days — I am writing about forty years ago — did not have the forests and plantations marked on them, or the reservoir. The iron in the rocks makes compasses erratic. The soldiers were Geordies, to whom Dartmoor was dangerously alien. I telephoned the Army camp at Okehampton: had they by any chance lost any soldiers? They had indeed. Clipped voices ordered, 'Bring out the six-ton trucks.' I tried to explain how to reach the lost soldiers, saying that there were many roads fanning out from the forest onto the moor and that they must enquire which to take from the keeper at the reservoir (an ex-Royal Marine Commando). The clipped voices would not listen.

Quite a number of search parties got lost that day. Six-ton trucks roaring through Chagford and up onto the moor aroused curiosity. Our barber, who was also the stringer for the newspapers, telephoned me. 'What's going on up there?' he asked. 'What's happening up your way?'

As my eldest son was in the Army I felt bound not to let on that the Durham Light Infantry was making a fool of itself. 'Oh, nothing,' I lied, 'nothing at all,' and still the six-ton trucks raced up onto the moor and vanished into Fernworthy Forest. At last came the exasperated colonel. I gave him a drink and he listened as I told him where his men were and how to find them. 'How many have you actually lost?' I asked, refilling his glass.

'Ninety-six,' he hissed, 'if you count the officers.'

All were found, a few frost-bitten, and none of them really

A moorland farm near
Headland Warren.

took to the moor, but a week later when we were still cut off
on top of the moor, enjoying the beauty of it all, the baker rang
up from the village. 'What's going on at Thornworthy? You having a wedding or something? The shop is full of flowers for you.'

'What's on the labels?' I asked.

'They say,' said the baker, '"with love from the Dumb Light
Infantry".'

Forty years on, they have helicopters.

Sheep grazing in lush
pastures above Cullaford.

# Inspired by a Sheep

I used to love riding out from Thornworthy Farm with Harold Wonnacott to round up his flock of black-faced sheep. Four or five of us and the dogs would circle the moor in a wide arc while the sheep bunched together to move in a fleecy mass towards the farm where, depending on the season, they would be dipped or shorn. Keeping packed together, bleating in unison, the flock would surge ahead of our horses, the boldest turning now and again to outface a sheepdog and stamp a foot, protecting her lamb. I have seen Harold, who had the ability to count his sheep at a glance, turn his horse about and ride back to where a frightened lamb had hidden, perhaps in the roots of a thorn. He would dismount, catch the lamb and rejoin the rest of us, the lamb in his arms.

Sheep are not stupid but they can have accidents and get into trouble like anybody else. When their fleeces are long, a scared sheep can get caught in the brambles and trapped. I have quite often run to get secateurs and clip a sheep free, and once when I was walking with my husband along the edge of a bog we saw in the black mud two amber eyes. A ewe, alarmed by something, had sprung sideways and sunk, trapped in the ooze. Struggling, she had gone under until only her eyes were visible. Lord knows how long she had been there.

A black-faced sheep has horns. My husband was able to grip them. I watched as he heaved and as the sheep with her mud-soaked fleece came up, his gumboots filled and he went down.

Sometimes a ewe, heavy with lamb, will roll on her back, get stuck and need to be righted. The trick is to heave her onto her feet, hold her until the blood which has rushed to her head is steady again, then let her go. It was the sight of a sheep in this position – seen from a train on my way to London when I was too craven myself to take any action – that made me speculate on what type of person, in what sort of mood, would have the nerve to stop the train and set the sheep upright.

As my train rushed on, I hoped the farmer would soon find the sheep. But the spectacle stayed in my mind and played on my conscience. It set me thinking and not long after I wrote my novel *An Imaginative Experience*, in which Julia does have the guts to stop the train and save the sheep, thus consoling my conscience by literary proxy.

# Fernworthy

Fernworthy reservoir is a short walk across the moor from Thornworthy. The reservoir – or, as we used to call it, the lake – was formed by building a dam across a long shallow valley through which the upper Teign flowed from its source on the moor. In the valley there had been a small farm which disappeared as the waters rose, covering the granite buildings.

When the dam was built the Forestry Commission planted a large pine forest which embraces half the lake and reaches for miles up the hill and over the moor. It is not difficult to imagine oneself in Bavaria. The lake has attracted wildfowl and ospreys now visit every year as they migrate. Birders can watch from a hide, and parking places and picnic tables are provided for visitors. When we lived at Thornworthy there was none of this sophistication; we usually had the lake to ourselves, though sometimes people came up to fish for the trout which never grew large because the feed was poor. We had a boat and from this one of my sons would fish all day in solitary peace.

Twice in the years we lived at Thornworthy there was a drought; the lake shrank and the last task of the day would be to move the boat closer to the dam where there was still water to float it. Then as the water diminished the ruins of the farm would appear: a lane leading to it, a stone bridge across the stream and the skeletons of a house and barns. Come autumn and rain, the lake would fill up again, the lane, the bridge and the farm would vanish and water would roar over the dam. No boats are allowed on the lake these days and I suspect that traces

*To his right, away from the path and below it was a long reservoir, silver from the rising moon slicing the black water. He jogged downhill to the water's edge. Folly drank. Hugh felt the temperature of the water. He listened. There was no sound other than faint rustling in the reeds.*

*His mother, he remembered, as he crouched with his hands in the water, had told him that in her youth, sent to Germany to learn the language, she had swum at night in the lakes. He remembered her voice.*

*'We swam naked, darling. If we rode we took off the saddles and swam the horses. We held on to their manes and they drew us along. It was poetry . . . You should try it some time in a lake at night.'*

*He took off his clothes and waded into the water, trying not to make a splash. Folly followed. They swam out together.*

Jumping the Queue

Fernworthy reservoir.

of the farm are gradually disappearing. The forest is in its prime and the Forestry Commission now plant other trees as well as pine when they harvest a swathe.

I often longed to swim in the reservoir. Its cool, clear, peaty water would have been as perfect to swim in as a Scottish loch, but swimming was of course not allowed. The nearest I ever got was in imagination, when I was writing *Jumping the Queue*. Hugh walks up onto the moor by night with the dog Folly and, finding a reservoir, swims. But I have known somebody who did swim in the reservoir. A very old friend, now long dead, had watched the dam being built and seen the Teign river, a small moorland stream at that point, gradually fill the valley and drown the little farm. She told me that she and her husband had found the lake irresistible and decided to swim. It could do no harm, they thought, as they were perfectly clean people who bathed every day. So, decently attired in bathing dress, they waded in and swam joyfully out. But alas, she told me, 'We were seen by the eagle-eyed waterman's wife from across the reservoir. She came out of their house and beat on a tin tray with a wooden spoon to warn us off.' In our day the waterman was an ex-Royal Marine Commando of great authority and we would not have dreamed of risking his wrath.

I have found Fernworthy a good place for butterflies as well as birds and it has always been a paradise for foxes. When the hunt came there were so many foxes that every hound hunted his own line and by the end of the day half the pack was lost. For a week afterwards smelly and weary hounds would turn up in our yard in ones and twos and we would telephone the kennels to come and retrieve them until all were gathered in. I never in all my time heard of a kill and it was said that the fox population felt so secure they slept above ground; certainly when I have met one when out riding it has hardly bothered to step to one side. But I was always careful to shut up my geese and chickens, and in the lambing season our neighbour would keep the flock close to the farmhouse.

Autumn colour in
Fernworthy Forest.

144

Peace on the water.

# A New Home in Combe

When we left Chagford we moved to the south side of
Dartmoor; Thornworthy, which we were leaving, had become
too large and costly to manage. Through friends we discovered
Cullaford Cottage in Combe, a little jewel though in need of
renovation. To reach it one turned down a very narrow lane by
a granite cross and a blasted oak. The cross had been found by
the hedger and ditcher where Cromwell's soldiers had thrown
it into the ditch; the monks of Buckfast re-erected it, for it had
marked the boundary of abbey land in the Middle Ages. The
oak is as old as time and hollow.

The cottage was stone, half thatched, half tiled, and so old
that it had no foundations, as we found when we put in drains,

LEFT
This cross was found
in a ditch where it had
lain since the Reformation.
The oak tree behind it is
probably the same age.

RIGHT
Our cottage from
the lane.

NEAR RIGHT
A pathway leading
out of Combe.

FAR RIGHT
Wisteria covering
the cottage.

for the roots of a huge wisteria went right through under the walls and came out the other side. There was an inexhaustible well of pure water, a large unkempt garden and a wood with a trout stream. We moved in in 1962 but, idyllic though it was, we were never as happy as we had been at Thornworthy. Eric was already ill and growing progressively depressed as illness prevented him working.

I wrote four books in that cottage. I would write in the mornings and afternoons, moving between the sitting room and the dining room. As I wrote the first two – *Speaking Terms* and *The Sixth Seal* – I read them to Eric in the evenings to keep him amused. He was enormously pleased when they were published, hugely generous.

*Speaking Terms* was an anti-hunting spoof, in which anti-blood-sport children connive with animals they have discovered can speak to sabotage the hunts. I was so nervous of what might be hunting neighbours that I adopted my nom de plume, shortening my grandmother's name Wellesley to Wesley. In the event nobody cared, I need not have bothered. When writing *Speaking Terms* I placed it roughly round our cottage and the river Dart; for *The Sixth Seal*, a fantasy novel for children, I imagined Thornworthy, Chagford and the Dartmoor I had loved and knew.

When Eric died I was blocked and could not write for years; it was a very bad time. I was left with a child still at school,

The wooded gorge from
Buckfast to Hexworthy
viewed from Holne Cott.

depressed and lonely. When I started writing again, well-meaning
people who passed by would often shout 'Are you all right?'
and I'd have to offer them coffee. That would be the end of
work for the day. Then suddenly I found myself hard at work
on something that turned into *Haphazard House*. I became
completely obsessed with this fairy story about death, in which
I tried to tell children that death is just another phase of life. The

The river Dart
below Holne.

characters grew so real to me that one Sunday at mass I found
myself praying hard for an old man, only to realize I was
praying for a character in my book. When I became aware
of what I was doing I burst out laughing, to the astonishment
of the congregation.

I was living alone by then, my youngest son having gone to
London, but I had a beloved dog from the RSPCA and a cat;

The river Dart, where I
swam with my dog Rose.

my dog Rose and I used to walk for miles on the moor and, when it was warm, swim. The summer of 1976 was very hot and Rose and I swam in the Dart every day, either in a long pool at Spitchwick where I watched ring ouzels or under a waterfall near Holne, or further out on the moor near Hexworthy. Before ten and after five I had the moor to myself; the trippers had gone home for their tea.

Still shocked by Eric's death, I wondered about suicide, not for myself but for others. It seemed an easy idea for the lonely. I had when young – I have no idea why – worked out a comfortable way to go: a hot day, warm sea, lonely beach, sleeping pills. From this came my novel *Jumping the Queue*, but though my agent sent this and *Haphazard House* to many publishers, we got nothing but refusals.

By 1981 I was so short of money I feared I would not be able to run my car and without a car I could not continue to live in Cullaford Cottage. I was too far from any shop. I decided to move into my local market town where I could get by without a car; regretfully I put the cottage on the market.

It was winter and I caught virulent flu from a friend's child. It turned into double bronchial pneumonia. The doctor came and suggested hospital where there was one bed left. I said no, for in hospital I would not be allowed to have my dog on my bed or a hot-water bottle. The doctor went back to his surgery and told his partner I was probably dying; his partner said I was tough.

I managed to croak into the telephone to my solicitor and house agent that the front door would be open and possible

Summer in the woods along the Dart at Spitchwick.

purchasers were welcome to walk in. So while I coughed and wheezed, people came to view. I'd hear them walk in: 'This is nice,' they'd say. 'What a lot of books!' 'Oh, more books!' 'Let's see what's upstairs.' Then they would open my door and find me apparently dying in bed. One delightful man was so moved by my plight that he offered to rush and get oxygen cylinders, saying, 'My wife will never believe this!' She didn't: he brought her to see me a few days later to prove he had not told a tall story.

Then some dead keen buyers arrived bearing flowers. I could read their thoughts: 'Will she live long enough to sign the contract?' I did and moved to Totnes, taking with me the unsold manuscripts of *Jumping the Queue* and *Haphazard House*.

*Strolling by the river, pausing to throw sticks for the dogs, hearing a water vole plop, watching it swim close to the bank then vanish, seeing the swirl and rise of secret trout in the bottle green water, Hebe counted herself fortunate . . .*

Harnessing Peacocks

LEFT
The Dart from Holne.

RIGHT
At Spitchwick, where
I swim.

A year later I wrote to someone whom I had met at Macmillan and to a friend of a friend at Dent, telling the one I had a novel, the other a children's book. Miraculously Dent loved *Haphazard House* and bought it, and at Macmillan James Hale, their head of fiction, liked *Jumping the Queue*. He has become a very dear friend who corrects my hopeless punctuation. He once sent a postcard: 'I see you have discovered the semi-colon.'

Perhaps I need not have sold my cottage? I still miss the sound of the river, the owls hooting at night, the song of the mistle thrush and the wind in the trees.

Stepping stones smoothed round by the
water. The Dart at Huccaby.

*I* sold my cottage and moved from Cullaford to Totnes in 1981. I bought a very tall house in a narrow street squeezed between a pub and a Gospel Hall. At weekends I was elevated by the sound of hymns and in the evenings by bibulous cheer from the pub. I found the convenience of crossing the street to buy my newspaper and having every shop within four minutes' walk an agreeable surprise after years of living many miles from the nearest centre.

I soon settled into town life, particularly enjoying market days when people from all around come into town to do their weekly shopping. I buy honey and free range eggs from Mrs Stevenson from Cornworthy, fruit and vegetables from Western House Organic Farm, and flowers, plants and bulbs from Roger

In my tiny garden
in Totnes.

ABOVE Totnes from the castle battlements.
BELOW Fore Street.

Market day in Totnes.

Everything from fresh produce and plants to exotic fabrics
and live entertainment can be found in the market.

Sclater or Lesley and Norman Thomas who are immensely knowledgeable and have a delightful dog called Molly. A van from Brixham supplies very fresh fish. When I have done my shopping I have a prowl round the antique, book and junk stalls. A lot of wonderful stalls which sold fresh farm produce have gone out of business since Safeways arrived on the outskirts of Totnes and these I sadly miss, but the spaces they occupied have been filled by exotic stalls selling jewellery, clothes both new and second-hand, saris from India and furniture. There is really nothing you cannot find in Totnes market if you have the patience to search.

After my first year in Totnes I began to get published so I was still able to run a car, and then by keeping my eyes and ears open I found the little house I live in now, hidden up a secret alley. I have a garden and total quiet apart from the bells

Market day is the social highlight of the week.

174

LEFT
The famous clock tower
which divides the High
Street from Fore Street.

RIGHT
Our traffic warden
waiting to pounce.

of St Mary's exquisite church, and on Fridays I need only walk through a passageway, cross the street and I am in the market.

When writing *Second Fiddle* I got inspiration from the market as a location, though none of my characters remotely resembles any of my friends who have stalls. Some day, however, Molly may find herself in print, together with a very fat cat which regularly helps itself at the petfood stall, pretending its owners starve it.

## Past and Present

Totnes has been a town for ever. In medieval times it had a good harbour and a Norman castle perched up the hill, but it really took off and became rich in the Elizabethan era. If you walk up its very steep main street, behind what might look like a shoe shop or an optician's you will find a house which is quintessentially Tudor, a rich merchant's house with beautiful moulded ceilings and huge stone fireplaces. There is a lovely church, St Mary's, and a Guildhall, and what I find particularly delightful is that no two houses are the same. Totnes really has only the one main street, the High Street which becomes Fore Street and climbs the hill to the castle. Off this street, like the bones of a herring, are numerous alleyways leading to little houses like mine and through to the two other streets, North Street and South Street, which follow the line of what were once the town walls.

Apart from London, I have never lived in a town in England but I think Totnes is exceptional. There is so much going on. I am not a joiner but if I wished there is drama and a lot of music. The annual music festival takes place a mile away at Dartington Hall (the Elmhursts of Dartington left their stamp on the neighbourhood), there are good concerts all year round, and since the early 1980s we have had the splendid literary festival run by Kay Dunbar and her husband. Dartington also has a cinema and shows all the most recherché films.

In the gardens at
Dartington Hall.

There are more painters, potters, writers, sculptors, photographers, film makers and musicians – actors too – to the square mile than can possibly be normal. They surely outnumber the Barbours and wellington boots! Again I suspect the Dartington influence.

In addition, Totnes has become something of a centre for alternative medicine. I lose count of the chiropractors, acupuncturists, reflexologists, masseurs, Alexander technicians, aromatherapists and other healers. This is quite apart from our excellent doctors and dentists and snug cottage hospital. We have, of course, a health food shop and we think we know all about organic food and the dreaded GM crops; in fact Totnes feels so strongly about the GM issue that it mustered the first posse in the country to sally forth and trash. (I regret that at the time I was unaware the trashing was planned, though I was with them in spirit.)

We also have fortune tellers and horoscope readers. The tang of the Middle Ages haunts the town, so that I wonder whether the trashing of a GM crop might call forth similar emotions to the dunking of a witch. I must do a little research in our friendly public library or in one of our excellent bookshops.

Come to think of it, I have toads in my garden and have spotted a newt in a friend's pond.

LEFT
A view of Totnes from the
playing fields showing
the church and the castle.

RIGHT
Fore Street and
High Street leading
up the hill to the castle.

# LOOKING AHEAD
## *A Greener Future*

A green lane leading to
secret villages and farms
along the Dart estuary.

When we first lived in Cornwall and later in Devon, the journey to Penzance or Chagford entailed driving through every town or village large or small en route from London. This could be entertaining, for we might stop for a drink or a meal or just to admire the view, but it was often frustrating as we were looking forward to arriving at our destination. I remember a friend exclaiming when he arrived, 'We drove so slowly through Exeter we could count every brick, the traffic was awful!' This was in the 1950s; since then, of course, bypasses have sprouted around almost every town and village.

In my youth the traffic was minimal compared to now. I vividly remember driving from London to Penzance in 1937, the night after George VI's Coronation, along silent empty roads passing through sleeping towns and villages all decked with bunting and Union Jacks. Now we have motorways that are busy night and day but curiously enough the journeys do not take less time.

These motorways have gobbled up an awful lot of agricultural land and the land too has changed, largely as a result of the intensive farming practices which have been developed since the Second World War. Now it is drenched with hormones, pesticides and fertilizers. A meadow is no longer a meadow, it is a field growing a crop of grass for silage, and so we have lost our wild flowers, insects, small mammals and birds. There is nothing

Bow Creek on the Dart estuary.

for them to eat, nowhere for the flowers to grow. I complain and so do many others. I am glad to say that people are waking up. If the organic farmers, the RSPB, the Council for the Protection of Rural England and the National Trust shout loud enough we will be heard. We need to be heard.

Oddly enough the motorways, whether you like it or not, are becoming a haven for wildlife. The Highway Department does not spray the verges, so they have become a sanctuary for flowers which used to grow in the fields and a perilous haven too for small mammals – field mice, moles, stoats and weasels – and even the fox, badger and rabbit. All these attract owls and kestrels, and one cannot drive far along a motorway without glimpsing a hovering kestrel (or, for that matter, without sighting a squashed fox or badger which has misjudged the traffic). I do not like to be too pessimistic, but it is difficult to be hopeful when experts such as David Attenborough utter such dire and tragic warnings about what man has done and continues to do to the planet. Instead of weeping and wailing, we should encourage the organic farmer, laud the Highway Department, and take an interest in the wonderful Eden Project near St Austell. We should visit the Lost Gardens of Heligan, now rediscovered and cultivated entirely on old-fashioned organic

BELOW AND RIGHT
The Eden Project coming to life in a disused china clay pit near St Austell. Within a series of biomes, the largest geodesic lean-to conservatories in the world, the project tells the story of human dependence on plants.

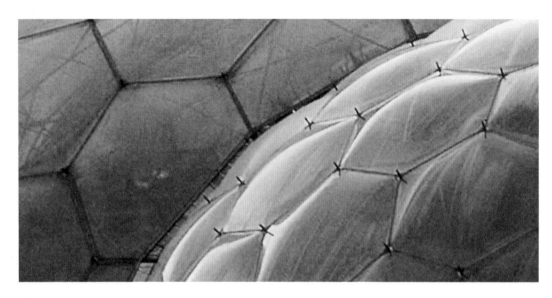

The windmills of Cornwall
make a dramatic
landscape.

*I shall plant woods of oak, beech, chestnut and among them flowering cherries. I will plant the cherries in curves and circles so that when some future airman flies over them he will see the name Calypso spelled out in blossom.*

The Camomile Lawn

Bluebells in spring.

lines, using lots of horse and cow dung. We should walk along the cliffs and riversides protected by the National Trust, help farmers to find ways to encourage and protect wild birds and, above all, educate our children to cherish what is still theirs.

Here in Devon we have a society to protect our hedges, which not only give food and shelter to birds and small mammals but are of great historical interest. Planted many hundreds of years ago, they can be dated by the number of species growing in them. We have woods full of bluebells and wild daffodils, snowdrops, violets and primroses, and some of the most beautiful rivers in England. Great stretches of cliffs stride along the Atlantic coast and the Bristol Channel, and of course there are the moors. Though much has changed since I first loved this land as a child of six the essence of the West Country is still here, and the spirit is here to keep it so. I have a friend who has the right attitude. He recently wrote, 'I have just planted five thousand beech trees. Come back and see them in two hundred and fifty years when they will be in their prime.'

By the river Dart at Whitestone.

# Acknowledgements

The page numbers given in bold below for the quotations from Mary Wesley's novels refer to this book. The italic numbers refer to the Black Swan editions of the novels.

From *The Camomile Lawn*:
**P. 15** 'Come, Ducks, run', *p. 135*;
**P. 20** Later, sitting in the sun, *p. 243*;
**P. 41** It must have been about here, *p. 287*;
**P. 49** A torch flashed three times, *p. 40*;
**P. 55** 'Shall we go and see', *p. 157*;
**P. 78** Sophy, home for the holidays, *p. 232*;
**P. 105** 'I walked,' said Polly, *p. 244*;
**P. 190** I shall plant woods of oak, *p. 188*.

From *Jumping the Queue*:
**P. 22** 'Like some maize?', *p. 7*;
**P. 88** All the way along the cliff path, *pp. 14-15*;
**P. 142** To his right, away from the path, *pp. 97-8*.

From *A Sensible Life*:
**P. 27** There was no wind, *p. 1*;
**P. 28** She crouched by the water's edge, *p. 119*;
**P. 101** Flora listened as she rode, *p. 176*.

From *Harnessing Peacocks*:
**P. 58** They were now tacking, *pp. 124-5*;
**P. 68** 'We go across here', *pp. 68-9*;

**P. 70** Giles looked round the room, *p. 71*;
**P. 94** The wind had dropped, *p. 160*;
**P. 98** 'Where have you been?', *p. 19*;
**P. 119** He parked his car, *p. 108*;
**P. 162** Strolling by the river, *p. 149*.

From *Part of the Furniture*:
**P. 106** What she saw was a stretch of moor, *p. 79*;
**P. 138** Juno murmured, 'Smells', *pp. 180-1*.

I am grateful to the Morrab Picture Library, Penzance, for permission to use the photograph of French crabbers on p. 79, and to Charles Francis for the use of his photographs of the Eden Project on pp. 188-9.

Thanks to James Long, whose enthusiasm and encouragement were so important; to Toby Eady for chivying us along; to the people of Totnes Market, to the fishermen of Newlyn, and to Jean Shrimpton of the Abbey Hotel (at last I got to photograph her). Thanks also to all the friends who let me photograph their land and gardens, drove boats and cars, held lambs and geese; and to Lady Silvia Sayer for her part in preserving Dartmoor. Our thanks to Judith Robertson for her brilliant design and perseverance, and to the team at Transworld, including Sally Gaminara, Deborah Adams and Alison Martin.                    *KS*